The human heart has hidden treasures . . .

—CHARLOTTE BRONTË

This book was given to

_____

by

_____

on

_____

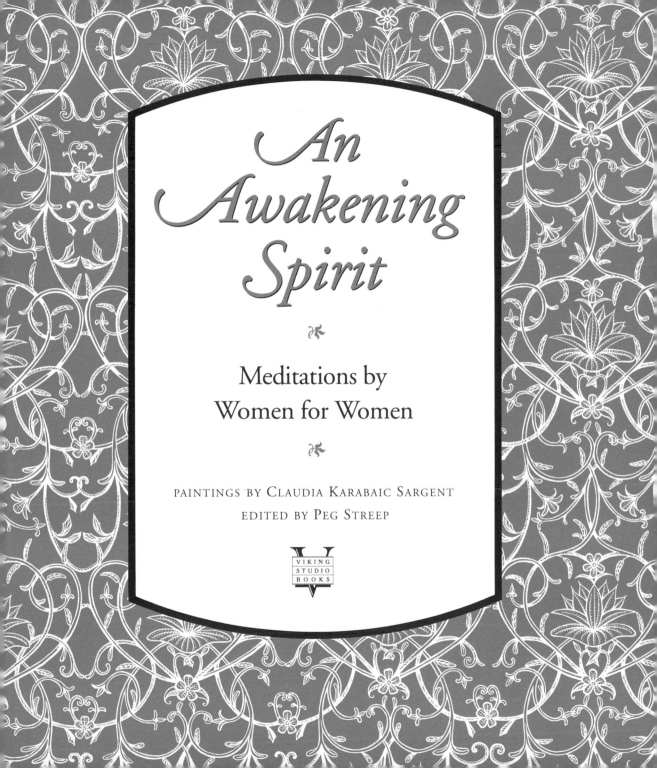

An Awakening Spirit

Meditations by
Women for Women

PAINTINGS BY CLAUDIA KARABAIC SARGENT
EDITED BY PEG STREEP

VIKING
STUDIO
BOOKS

For my nieces, Alyssa Angela Kaporch and Amanda Nicole Karabaic, with all my love;
may you be inspired by the lives of your foremothers to blossom into the strong, wise, brave,
and beautiful women I know you are destined to become.
—C.K.S.

For Alexandra, whose spirit already contains the woman within, and for Peter,
who awakened my spirit.
—P.S.

VIKING STUDIO BOOKS
Published by the Penguin Group
Penguin Books USA Inc., 375 Hudson Street, New York, New York 10014, U.S.A.
Penguin Books Ltd, 27 Wrights Lane, London W8 5TZ, England
Penguin Books Australia Ltd, Ringwood, Victoria, Australia
Penguin Books Canada Ltd, 10 Alcorn Avenue, Toronto, Ontario, Canada M4V 3B2
Penguin Books (N.Z.) Ltd, 182–190 Wairau Road, Auckland 10, New Zealand

Penguin Books Ltd, Registered Offices: Harmondsworth, Middlesex, England

First American Edition
Published in 1993 by Viking Penguin, a division of Penguin Books USA Inc.
1 3 5 7 9 10 8 6 4 2
Copyright © Peg Streep, 1993
Illustrations copyright © Claudia Karabaic Sargent, 1993
All rights reserved

Pages 108–110 constitute an extension of this copyright page.

LIBRARY OF CONGRESS CATALOGING IN PUBLICATION DATA
An Awakening spirit: meditations by women for women/paintings by
Claudia Karabaic Sargent; edited by Peg Streep.
p. cm.
ISBN 0-670-84887-5
1. Meditations. 2. Women—Prayer-books and devotions—English.
I. Streep, Peg.
BL625.7.A93 1993
291.4'3—dc20   93-6472

Printed in Japan
Set in Adobe Garamond and Centaur
Typography for interior and slip case by Kathryn Parise

Introduction

"Awakening." This wonderful, rather old-fashioned word summons up images of warm sheets, tousled hair, eyes momentarily blinded by the brightness of a new day. Unlike the rising of the sun, though, the awakenings of the spirit come at no appointed hour, nor at a specific chronological age. They have a rhythm and point of origin that are as unique as the individual herself. What they have in common are the moments of clarity and purpose they bequeath us, a vision of self and a sureness that we are following our hearts and minds.

An Awakening Spirit sets before us moments that have shaped women's lives. In poetry and prose, the voices here describe awakenings that find their beginnings in a childhood memory, in politics, in painting or writing, in loving, or in giving birth. Even personal catastrophe—the death of a loved parent or spouse—may define the self and the spirit within.

While all the voices presented here are those of women, the selections remind us that the experience of being female is as varied as the glorious multiplicity of the natural world. They tell us, too, that the achievement of the self, the full flowering of the spirit within, is often achieved only with effort, and sometimes at great cost. We hear this in Emily Dickinson's cry for escape from the boundaries of the self; in Marge Piercy's brilliant and moving poem "Looking at Quilts," about women's need to create amid the tedious routines of daily life; in Anne Morrow Lindbergh's struggle to be wife, mother, writer. We marvel at the extraordinary strength and self-reliance that comes with doing: in Elinore Pruitt Stewart's success as a pioneer homesteader, in Maya Angelou's achievement of motherhood, in Muriel Rukeyser's evocation of painting in "Cave Painters." And then there is the flowering and fortitude that comes from the extension of the self by loving: loving parents, sisters, brothers, children, lovers, husbands, friends.

The individual spirit may find its moment of awakening in the wash of color on canvas, in the sun-lit glory of a garden, in a passionate embrace, in the sweet-smelling skin of a child, or even in the solitude of an empty room. *All* are glorious. We hope *An Awakening Spirit* provides a place where you may see your own awakenings mirrored and brought to life.

—PEG STREEP

Contents

Self ❧ 12

Challenge ❧ 34

I thank all who have loved me in their hearts
  with thanks and love from mine. Deep thanks to all
Who paused a little near the prison wall
To hear my music in its louder parts . . .

—ELIZABETH BARRETT BROWNING

Self

You may then wonder where they have gone, those other dim dots that were you: you in the flesh swimming in a swift river, swinging a bat on the first pitch, opening a footlocker with a screwdriver, inking and painting clowns on celluloid, stepping out of a revolving door into the swift crowd on a sidewalk, being kissed and kissing till your brain grew smooth, stepping out of the cold woods into a warm field full of crows, or lying awake in bed aware of your legs and suddenly aware of all of it, that the ceiling above you was under the sky—in what country, what town?

You may wonder, that is, as I sometimes wonder privately, but it doesn't matter. For it is not you or I that is important, neither what sort we might be nor how we came to be each where we are. What is important is anyone's coming awake and discovering a place, finding in full orbit a spinning globe one can lean over, catch, and jump on. What is important is the moment of opening a life and feeling it

touch—with an electric hiss and cry—this speckled mineral sphere, our present world.

On your mountain slope now you must take on faith that those apparently discrete dots of you were contiguous: that little earnest dot, so easily amused; that alien, angry adolescent; and this woman with loosening skin on bony hands, hands now fifteen years older than your mother's hands when you pinched their knuckle skin into mountain ridges on an end table. You must take on faith that those severed places cohered, too—the dozens of desks, bedrooms, kitchens, yards, landscapes—if only through the motion and shed molecules of the traveler. You take it on faith that the multiform and variously lighted latitudes and longitudes were part of one world, that you didn't drop chopped from house to house, coast to coast, life to life, but in some once comprehensible way moved there, a city block at a time, a highway mile at a time . . .

—ANNIE DILLARD

When we have not come into ourselves we say, in solitude: "No one loves me; I am alone." When we have chosen solitude, we say: "Thank God, I am alone!"

—LOUISE BOGAN

You can live a lifetime and, at the end of it, know more about other people than you know about yourself. You learn to watch other people, but you never watch yourself because you strive against loneliness. If you read a book, or shuffle a deck of cards, or care for a dog, you are avoiding yourself. The abhorrence of loneliness is as natural as wanting to live at all. If it were otherwise, men would never have bothered to make an alphabet, nor to have fashioned words out of what were only animal sounds, nor to have crossed continents—each man to see what the other looked like.

Being alone in an aeroplane for even so short a time as a night and a day, irrevocably alone, with nothing to observe but your instruments and your own hands in semi-darkness, nothing to contemplate but the size of your small courage, nothing to wonder about but the beliefs, the faces, and the hopes rooted in your mind—such an experience can be as startling as the first awareness of a stranger walking by your side at night. You are the stranger.

—BERYL MARKHAM

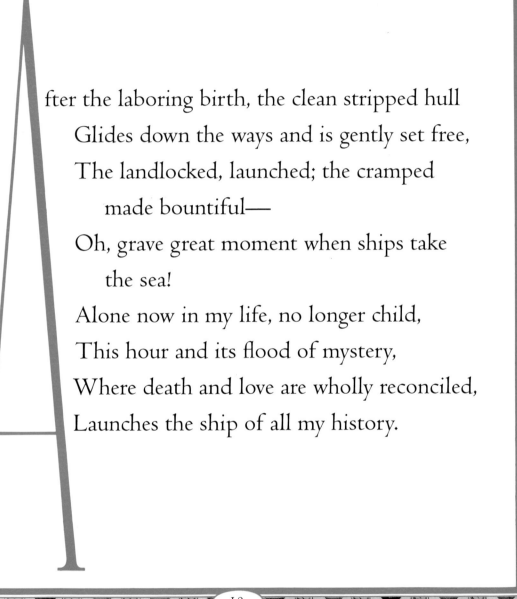

After the laboring birth, the clean stripped hull
    Glides down the ways and is gently set free,
    The landlocked, launched; the cramped
        made bountiful—
    Oh, grave great moment when ships take
      the sea!
    Alone now in my life, no longer child,
    This hour and its flood of mystery,
    Where death and love are wholly reconciled,
    Launches the ship of all my history.

Accomplished now is the last struggling birth,
I have slipped out from the embracing shore
Nor look for comfort to maternal earth.
I shall not be a daughter any more,
But through this final parting, all stripped down,
Launched on the tide of love, go out full grown.

—MAY SARTON

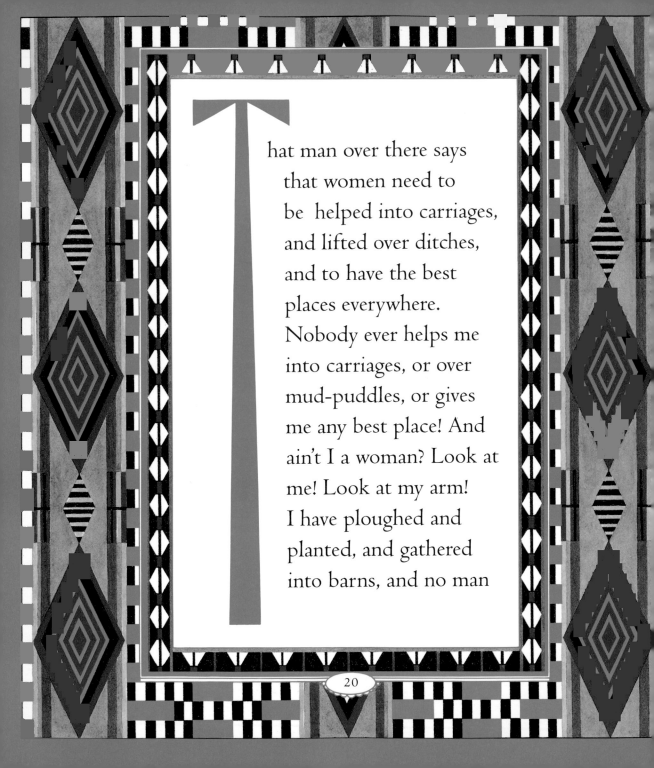

That man over there says that women need to be helped into carriages, and lifted over ditches, and to have the best places everywhere. Nobody ever helps me into carriages, or over mud-puddles, or gives me any best place! And ain't I a woman? Look at me! Look at my arm! I have ploughed and planted, and gathered into barns, and no man

could head me! And ain't I
a woman? I could work as
much and eat as much as
a man—when I could get
it—and bear the lash as
well! And ain't I a woman?
I have borne thirteen
children, and seen them
most all sold off to slavery,
and when I cried out with
my mother's grief, none
but Jesus heard me! And
ain't I a woman?

—Sojourner Truth

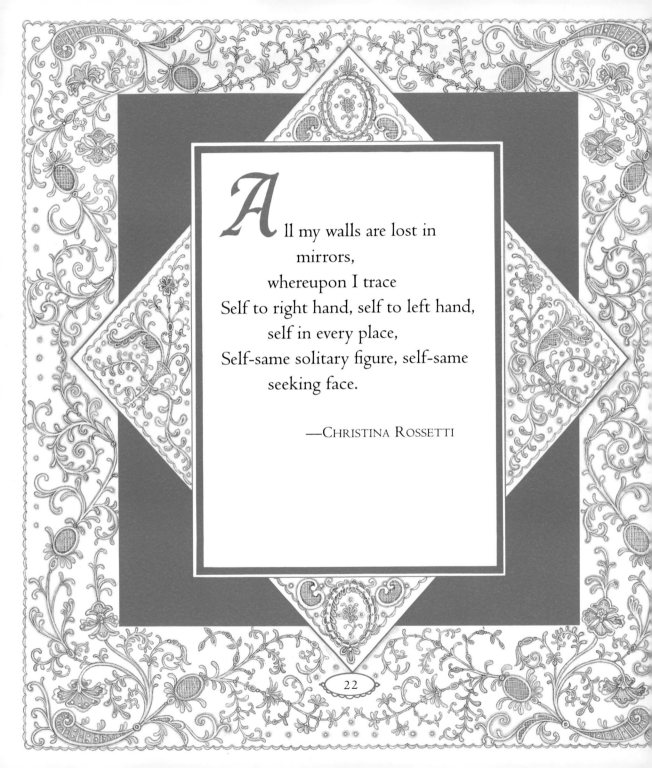

*A*ll my walls are lost in
mirrors,
whereupon I trace
Self to right hand, self to left hand,
self in every place,
Self-same solitary figure, self-same
seeking face.

—CHRISTINA ROSSETTI

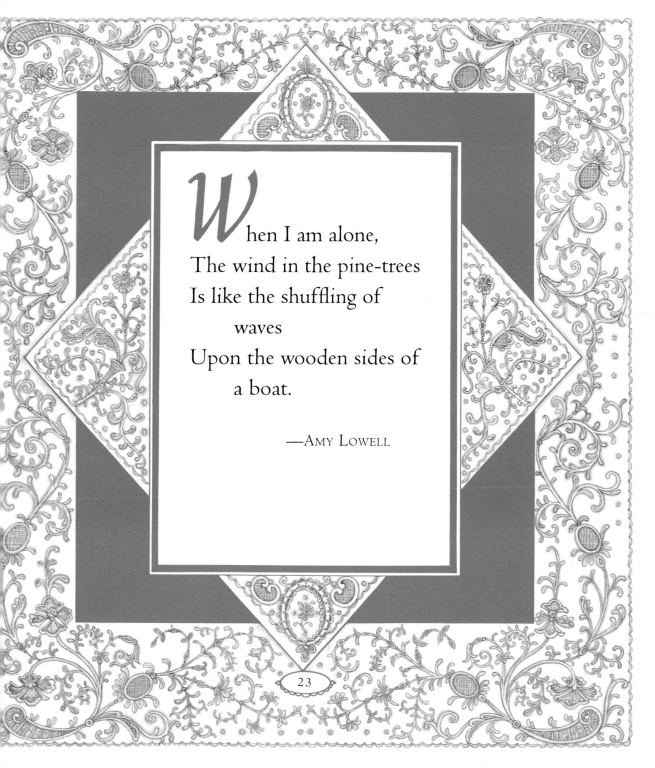

When I am alone,
The wind in the pine-trees
Is like the shuffling of
waves
Upon the wooden sides of
a boat.

—AMY LOWELL

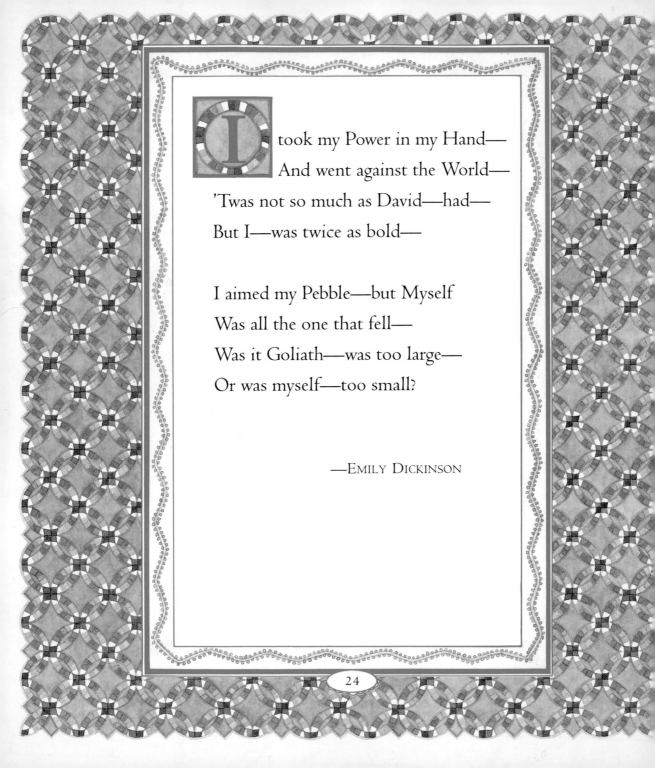

I took my Power in my Hand—
And went against the World—
'Twas not so much as David—had—
But I—was twice as bold—

I aimed my Pebble—but Myself
Was all the one that fell—
Was it Goliath—was too large—
Or was myself—too small?

—EMILY DICKINSON

24

That night she was like the little tottering, stumbling, clutching child, who of a sudden realizes its powers, and walks for the first time alone, boldly and with over-confidence. She could have shouted for joy. She did shout for joy, as with a sweeping stroke or two she lifted her body to the surface of the water.

A feeling of exultation overtook her, as if some power of significant import had been given her to control the working of her body and her soul. She grew daring and reckless, overestimating her strength. She wanted to swim far out, where no woman had swum before.

—KATE CHOPIN

"Oh, it is difficult—life is very difficult! It seems right to me sometimes that we should follow our strongest feeling; but then, such feelings continually come across the ties that all our former life has made for us—the ties that have made others dependent on us—and would cut them in two. If life were quite easy and simple, as it might have been in Paradise, and we could always see that one being first towards whom . . . I mean, if life did not make duties for us before love comes—love would be a sign that two people ought to belong to each other. But I see—I feel it is not so now: there are things we must renounce in life: some of us must resign love. Many things are difficult and dark to me; but I see one thing quite clearly—that I must not, cannot seek my own happiness by sacrificing others."

—GEORGE ELIOT

The days grow and the stars cross over

And my wild bed turns slowly among the stars.

—MURIEL RUKEYSER

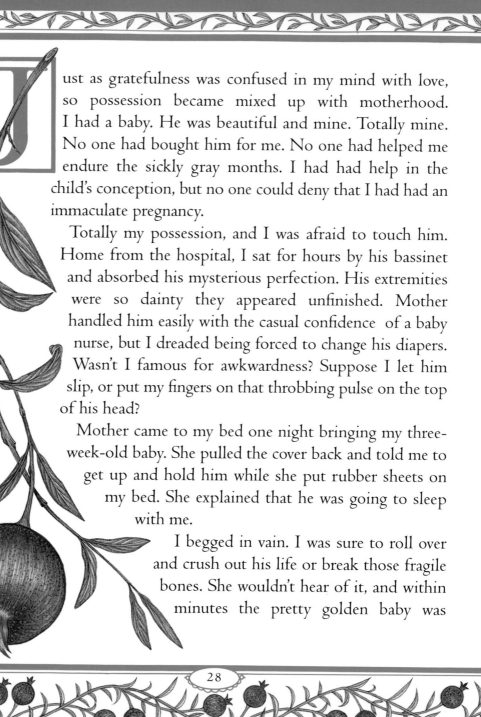

ust as gratefulness was confused in my mind with love, so possession became mixed up with motherhood. I had a baby. He was beautiful and mine. Totally mine. No one had bought him for me. No one had helped me endure the sickly gray months. I had had help in the child's conception, but no one could deny that I had had an immaculate pregnancy.

Totally my possession, and I was afraid to touch him. Home from the hospital, I sat for hours by his bassinet and absorbed his mysterious perfection. His extremities were so dainty they appeared unfinished. Mother handled him easily with the casual confidence of a baby nurse, but I dreaded being forced to change his diapers. Wasn't I famous for awkwardness? Suppose I let him slip, or put my fingers on that throbbing pulse on the top of his head?

Mother came to my bed one night bringing my three-week-old baby. She pulled the cover back and told me to get up and hold him while she put rubber sheets on my bed. She explained that he was going to sleep with me.

I begged in vain. I was sure to roll over and crush out his life or break those fragile bones. She wouldn't hear of it, and within minutes the pretty golden baby was lying on his back in the center of my bed, laughing at me.

I lay on the edge of the bed, stiff with fear, and vowed not to sleep all night long. But the eat-sleep routine I had begun in the hospital, and kept up under Mother's dictatorial command, got the better of me. I dropped off.

My shoulder was shaken gently. Mother whispered, "Maya, wake up. But don't move."

I knew immediately that the awakening had to do with the baby. I tensed. "I'm awake."

She turned the light on and said, "Look at the baby." My fears were so powerful I couldn't move to look at the center of the bed. She said again, "Look at the baby." I didn't hear sadness in her voice, and that helped me to break the bonds of terror. The baby was no longer in the center of the bed. At first I thought he had moved. But after closer investigation I found that I was lying on my stomach with my arm bent at a right angle. Under the tent of blanket, which was poled by my elbow and forearm, the baby slept touching my side.

Mother whispered, "See, you don't have to think about doing the right thing. If you're for the right thing, then you do it without thinking."

She turned out the light and I patted my son's body lightly and went back to sleep.

—Maya Angelou

29

$\mathcal{Y}$es, and I long for one thing more: to learn how to listen to the delicate vibrations of my soul, to be incorruptibly *true to myself* and fair to others, to find in this way the right measure of my own worth.

—Karen Horney

I have the fervour
of myself for a presence
and my own spirit for
light . . .

—H. D.

I think what is happening to me is so wonderful, and not only what can be seen on my body, but all that is taking place inside. I never discuss myself or any of these things with anybody; that is why I have to talk to myself about them. Each time I have a period—and that has only been three times—I have the feeling that in spite of all the pain, unpleasantness, and nastiness, I have a sweet secret, and that is why, although it is nothing but a nuisance to me in a way, I always long for the time that I shall feel that secret within me again.

—ANNE FRANK

I accept the universe . . .

—Margaret Fuller

With stammering lips and insufficient sound,
I strive and struggle to deliver right
the music of my nature . . .

—Elizabeth Barrett Browning

Challenge

*i*n the house with the tortoise chair
    she will give birth to the pearl
        to the beautiful
          feather

in the house of the goddess who sits on a
    tortoise
    she will give birth to the necklace of
      pearls
        to the beautiful feathers
        we are

there she sits on the tortoise
    swelling to give us birth

on your way on your way
child be on your way to me here
you whom I made new

come here child   come be pearl
be beautiful feather

—Anonymous Native American (Aztec)
Translated by Anselm Hollo

No coward soul is mine
No trembler in the
world's storm-
troubled sphere
I see Heaven's glories
shine
And Faith shines
equal arming me
from Fear.

—EMILY BRONTË

38

Pain is the great teacher. I woke before dawn with this thought. Joy, happiness, are what we take and do not question. They are beyond question, maybe. A matter of being. But pain forces us to think, and to make connections, to sort out what is what, to discover what has been happening to cause it. And, curiously enough, pain draws us to other human beings in a significant way, whereas joy or happiness to some extent, isolates.

—May Sarton

My mother has stopped talking. She raises her eyebrows, asking me to respond to her. Soon I know if I hold silence she will take a deep breath and straighten her shoulders. "Daughter," she will say, in a voice that is stern and admonishing, "always a woman must be stronger than the most terrible circumstance. You know what my mother used say? Through us, the women of the world, only through us can everything survive."

An image comes to me. I see

generations of women bearing a flame. It is hidden, buried deep within, yet they are handing it down from one to another, burning. It is a gift of fire, transported from a world far off and far away, but never extinguished. And now, in this very moment, my mother imparts the care of it to me. I must keep it alive, I must manage not to be consumed by it, I must hand it on when the time comes to my daughter.

—Kim Chernin

I never hear the word "escape"
  Without a quicker blood,
  A sudden expectation,
  A flying attitude!

I never hear of prisons broad
  By soldiers battered down,
  But I tug childish at my bars
  Only to fail again!

—EMILY DICKINSON

When I was a good and quick little
    girl
they treated me like a treasure

oh heart!

Many suns and many moons I saw
time passes

oh heart!

How I have changed. I am not a girl
    now
I am very old

oh heart!

What is the use of grieving
if nobody will listen

oh heart!

—ANONYMOUS NATIVE AMERICAN (PAMPA)
Translated by W. S. Merwin

Who is this cross old woman for whom I can do nothing right? I don't know her. She is not my mother. I am not her daughter. She won't eat anything I cook, so we resort to games. I do the cooking as usual—and I'm quite a good cook; it's one of my few domestic virtues, and the only part of housekeeping which I enjoy—and someone will say, "Eat Alan's soup, Grandmother. You know you like Alan's soup." Or, "Have some of Hugh's delicious salad." She won't eat the salad, when Hugh is in New York, until we tell her that Hugh made the dressing before he left.

I know that it is a classic symptom of atherosclerosis, this turning against the person you love most, and this knowledge

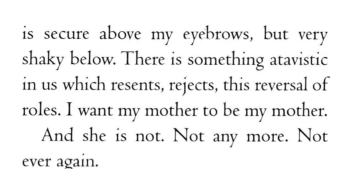

is secure above my eyebrows, but very shaky below. There is something atavistic in us which resents, rejects, this reversal of roles. I want my mother to be my mother.

And she is not. Not any more. Not ever again.

I go searching for her.

My first memories of her are early, and are memories of smell, that oft-neglected sense, which is perhaps the first sense we use fully. Mother always smelled beautiful. I remember burrowing into her neck just for the soft loveliness of scented skin.

After smell came sound, the sound of her voice, singing to me, talking. I took the beauty of her voice for granted until I was almost grown up.

Scent. Sound. Vision.

—MADELEINE L'ENGLE

The art of losing isn't hard to master;
so many things seem filled with the intent
to be lost that their loss is no disaster.

Lose something every day. Accept the fluster
of lost door keys, the hour badly spent.
The art of losing isn't hard to master.

Then practice losing farther, losing faster:
places, and names, and where it was you meant
to travel. None of these will bring disaster.

I lost my mother's watch. And look! my last, or
next-to-last, of three loved houses went.
The art of losing isn't hard to master.

I lost two cities, lovely ones. And, vaster,
some realms I owned, two rivers, a continent.
I miss them, but it wasn't a disaster.

—Even losing you (the joking voice, a gesture
I love) I shan't have lied. It's evident
the art of losing's not too hard to master
though it may look like (*Write* it!) like disaster.

—ELIZABETH BISHOP

I so liked Spring last year
    Because you were here;—
    The thrushes too—
Because it was these you so
    liked to hear—
    I so liked you.

This year's a different thing,—
    I'll not think of you.
But I'll like Spring because it is
    simply Spring
    As the thrushes do.

—Charlotte Mew

m y boat goes west, yours east
    heaven's a wind for both
        journeys
    from here the clouds and
        mountains
    the horizon's vague
    a thousand miles
    my heart, a dark swan
    confused in that vastness

—CHAO LI-HUA
Translated by J. P. Seaton

49

The last day of what has been an uneasy and painful year for me. I look forward to dawn tomorrow and, as the days get longer, to begin to feel my way into renascence. It is not strange though it is mysterious that our "New Year" comes at the darkest time in the seasonal cycle. When there is personal darkness, when there is pain to be overcome, when we are forced to renew ourselves against all the odds, the psychic energy required simply to survive has tremendous force, as great as that of a bulb pushing up through icy ground in spring, so after the overcoming, there is extra energy, a flood of energy that can go into creation.

—MAY SARTON

And then, looking back over my life, a succession of "losts." My own baby, and Amelia Earhart and Nelson and Phil and many others. I know the pattern well—the first shock, then the false hopes, and time passing, passing. There is never any answer—just time passing. The person you love is a hostage, a hostage to fate. One pictures the worst horrors and one is powerless to do anything about it, even to hope, even to pray. Even my prayers seem to bounce back to me as though there were an impenetrable wall. Does one pray for the dead?

And yet the wall seems to have cracks in it sometimes, as it has in life. That night I lay under the elm tree in North Haven and looked up at the stars shining through its bare branches, so beautiful, the elm's bare branches, fruited with stars, hung with the heavens. The heavens, milky with the brilliance of many stars, veined with the dark branches of the elm. And there was a shooting star—right across the heavens— tearing it in half, ripping a great white gash in it.

—ANNE MORROW LINDBERGH

Courage is the price that life exacts for granting peace.

The soul that knows it not, knows no release

From little things;

Knows not the livid loneliness of fear,

Nor mountain heights where bitter joy can hear

The sound of wings.

—AMELIA EARHART

Would it not take one
　　Who slept alone to know it?
　　Who could have told you
　　That the nights in autumn
　　Are indeed extremely long?

　　　　　—TAKASHINA KISHI

I knew of a man who was sent to the State Prison for twenty-five years. All these years he was always thinking of his home, and counting the time till he should be free. The years roll on, the time of imprisonment is over, the man is free. He leaves the prison gates, he makes his way to the old home, but his old home is not there. The house in which he had dwelt in his childhood had been torn down, and a new one had been put in its place; his family was gone, their very name was forgotten, there was no one to take him by the hand to welcome him back to life.

So it was with me. I had crossed the line of which I had so long been dreaming. I was free; but there was no one to welcome me to the land of freedom, I was a stranger in a strange land, and my home after all was down in the old cabin quarter, with the old folks and my brothers and sisters. But to this solemn resolution I came; I was free, and they should be free also; I would make a home for them in the North, and the Lord helping me, I would bring them all there.

—HARRIET TUBMAN

*W*hen I attain to utter forth in verse
    Some inward thought, my soul throbs audibly
    Along my pulses, yearning to be free
    And something farther, fuller, higher . . .

          —Elizabeth Barrett Browning

Creation

ho decided what is useful in its beauty
means less than what has no function besides beauty
(except its weight in money)?
Art without frames: it held parched corn,
it covered the table where soup misted savor,
it covered the bed where the body knit
to self and other and the
dark wool of dreams.

The love of the ordinary blazes out: the backyard
miracle: Ohio Sunflower,
Snail's Track,
Sweet Gum Leaf,
Moon over the Mountain.

In the pattern Tulip and Peony the sense
of design masters the essence of what sprawled

in the afternoon: called conventionalized
to render out the choice, the graphic wit.

Some have a wistful faded posy yearning:

                                       Star of the Four Winds,
                Star of the West,
                      Queen Charlotte's Crown.
In a crabbed humor as far from pompous
as a rolling pin, you can trace wrinkles
from smiling under a scorching grasshopper sun:
                Monkey Wrench,
                          The Drunkard's Path,
                                    Fool's Puzzle,
                  Puss in the Corner,
                        Robbing Peter to Pay Paul,
and the deflating
                  Hearts and Gizzards.

Pieced quilts, patchwork from best gowns,
winter woolens, linens, blankets, worked jigsaw
of the memories of braided lives, precious
scraps: women were buried but their clothing wore on.

Out of death from childbirth at sixteen, hard
work at forty, out of love for the trumpet vine
and the melon, they issue to us:

Rocky Road to Kansas,

Job's Troubles,

Crazy Ann,

The Double Irish Chain,

The Tree of Life:

this quilt might be

the only perfect artifact a woman
would ever see, yet she did not doubt
what we had forgotten, that out of her
potatoes and colic, sawdust and blood
she could create; together, alone,
she seized her time and made new.

—MARGE PIERCY

But you ask too much, I want to cry out. I cannot be having a baby and be a good housekeeper and keep thinking and writing on the present times (in my diary) and be always free to discuss anything with you and give to the children and keep an atmosphere of peace in the family (the bigger family which is so scattered and distraught now, all of us disagreeing) and keep my mind clear and open on the present-day things and write a book at the same time. I cannot be an efficient woman and house-manager *and* an artist at the same time.

Throw in a baby and it takes all your extra strength as well as all the creative urge in you. Once the baby starts to move and you are physically conscious of what you are creating you can no longer create in another line, at least *not* to your best capacity. I think I feel this so strongly that it is really what keeps me from writing. I know it will *not* be the best writing. The *best* writing is going into that child.

—ANNE MORROW LINDBERGH

Child who within me gives me dreams and sleep,

Your sleep, your dreams: you hold me in your flesh

Including me where nothing has included

Until I said   :   I will include, will wish

And in my belly be a birth, will keep

All delicacy, all delight unclouded.

Dreams of an unborn child move through my dreams,

The sun is not alone in making fire and wave

Find meeting-place, for flesh and future meet,

The seal in the green wave like you in me,

Child.   My blood at night full of your dreams,

Sleep coming by day as strong as sun on me,

Coming with sun-dreams where leaves and rivers

    meet,

And I at last alive sunlight and wave.

—MURIEL RUKEYSER

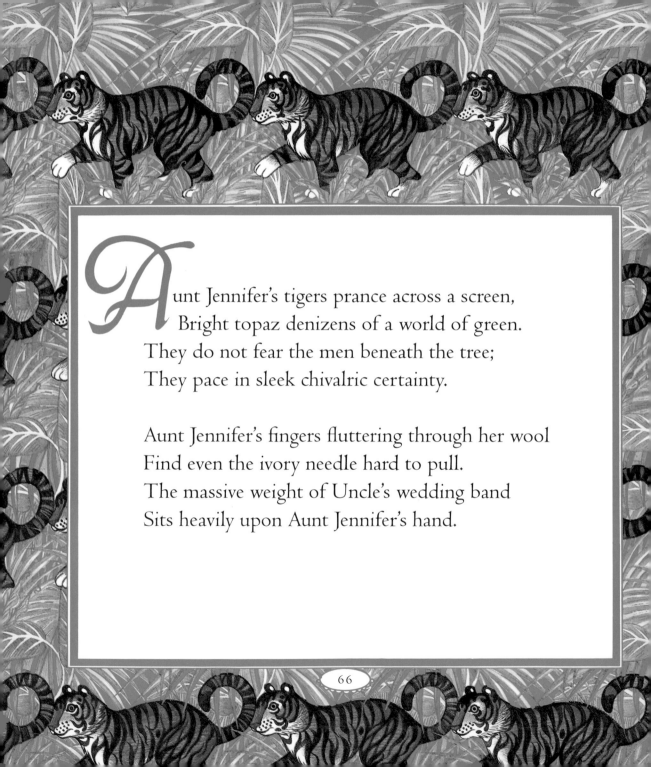

Aunt Jennifer's tigers prance across a screen,
Bright topaz denizens of a world of green.
They do not fear the men beneath the tree;
They pace in sleek chivalric certainty.

Aunt Jennifer's fingers fluttering through her wool
Find even the ivory needle hard to pull.
The massive weight of Uncle's wedding band
Sits heavily upon Aunt Jennifer's hand.

When Aunt is dead, her terrified hands will lie
Still ringed with ordeals she was mastered by.
The tigers in the panel that she made
Will go on prancing, proud and unafraid.

—ADRIENNE RICH

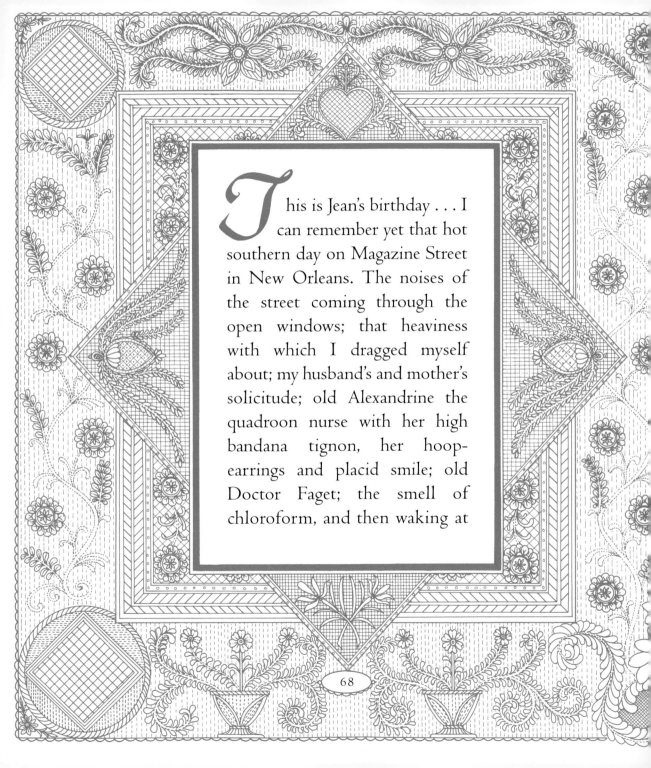

This is Jean's birthday . . . I can remember yet that hot southern day on Magazine Street in New Orleans. The noises of the street coming through the open windows; that heaviness with which I dragged myself about; my husband's and mother's solicitude; old Alexandrine the quadroon nurse with her high bandana tignon, her hoop-earrings and placid smile; old Doctor Faget; the smell of chloroform, and then waking at

68

six in the evening from out of a stupor to see in my mother's arms a little piece of humanity all dressed in white which they told me was my little son! The sensation with which I touched my lips and my finger tips to his soft flesh only comes once to a mother. It must be pure animal sensation; nothing spiritual could be so real—so poignant.

—KATE CHOPIN

The greatest gift of a garden is the restoration of the five senses.

During the first year in the country I noticed but few birds, the second year I saw a few more, but by the fourth year the air, the tree tops, the thickets and ground seemed teeming with bird life. "Where did they all suddenly come from?" I asked myself. The birds had always been there, but I hadn't the power to see; I had been made purblind by the city and only gradually regained my power of sight.

My ears, deafened by the ceaseless whir and din of commerce, had lost the keenness which catches the nuances of bird melody, and it was long before I was aware of distinguishing the varying tones that afterward meant joy, sorrow, loss or love, to me. That hearing has now become so keen, there is no bond of sleep so strong that the note of a strange bird will not pierce to the unsleeping, subconscious ear and arouse me instantly to alertness in every fibre of my being. I wonder if even death will make me insensate to the first chirp of a vanguard robin in March. . . .

The delicacy of touch comes back gradually by tending injured birdlings, by the handling of fragile infant plants, and by the acquaintance with different leaf textures, which finally makes one able to distinguish a plant, even in the dark, by its Irish tweed, silken or fur finish.

And the foot, how intangibly it becomes sensitized; how instinctively it avoids a plant even when the eye is busy elsewhere. On the darkest night I can traverse the rocky ravine, the thickets, the sinuous paths through overgrown patches, and never stumble, scratch myself or crush a leaf. My foot knows every unevenness of each individual bit of garden, and adjusts itself lovingly without conscious thought of brain.

To the ears that have learned to catch the first tentative lute of a marsh frog in spring, orchestras are no longer necessary. To the eyes that have regained their sight, more wonder lies in the craftsmanship of a tiny leaf-form of inconsequential weed, than is to be found in bombastic arras. To the resuscitated nose is revealed the illimitable secrets of earth incense, the whole gamut of flower perfume, and other fragrant odors too intangible to be classed, odors which wing the spirit to realms our bodies are as yet too clumsy to inhabit.

To the awakened mind there is nothing so lowly in the things below and above ground but can command respect and study. Darwin spent only thirty years on the study of the humble earthworm. . . .

Garden making is creative work, just as much as painting or writing a poem. It is a personal expression of self, an individual conception of beauty.

—HANNA RION

71

In the cave with a long-ago flare
a woman stands, her arm up. Red twig, black twig,
   brown twig.
A wall of leaping darkness over her.
The men are out hunting in the early light
But here in this flicker, one or two men, painting
and a woman among them.

Great living animals grow on the stone walls,
their pelts, their eyes, their sex, their hearts,
and the cave-painters touch them with life, red,
  brown, black,
a woman among them, painting.

—Muriel Rukeyser

A woman's voice, like the wind, rushes—
   Nocturnal it seems, moist and black,
   And as it flies, whatever it brushes
   Changes and will not change back.
   Its diamond-shine comes to bathe
      and bless,
   Things are draped in a silver light,
   It rustles its suggestive dress,

Woven of fantasy, silken and bright.
And the power that propels the
　　enchanted
Voice displays such hidden might,
It's as if the grave were not ahead,
But mysterious stairs beginning their
　　flight.

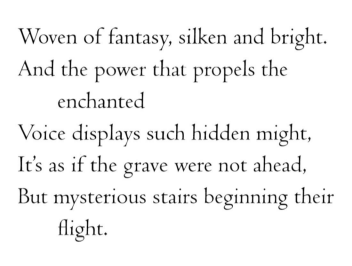

—ANNA AKHMATOVA

75

I never did like to theorize, and so this year I set out to prove that a woman could ranch if she wanted to. We like to grow potatoes on new ground, that is, newly cleared land on which no crop has been grown. Few weeds grow on new land, so it makes less work. So I selected my potato-patch, and the man ploughed it, although I could have done that if Clyde would have let me. I cut the potatoes, Jerrine helped, and we dropped them in the rows. The man covered them, and that ends the man's part. By that time the garden ground was ready, so I planted the garden. I had almost an acre in vegetables. I irrigated and I cultivated it myself.

We had all the vegetables we could possibly use, and now Jerrine and I have put in our cellar full, and this is what we have: one large bin of potatoes (more than two tons), half a ton of carrots, a large bin of beets, one of turnips, one of onions, one of parsnips, and on the other side of the cellar we have more than one hundred heads of cabbage. I have experimented and found a kind of squash that can be raised here, and that the ripe ones keep well and make good pies; also that the young tender ones make splendid pickles, quite equal to cucumbers. I was glad to stumble on

to that, because pickles are hard to manufacture when you have nothing to work with. Now I have plenty. They told me when I came that I could not even raise common beans, but I tried and succeeded. And also I raised lots of green tomatoes, and, as we like them preserved, I made them all up that way. Experimenting along another line, I found that I could make catchup, as delicious as that of tomatoes, of gooseberries. I made it exactly the same as I do the tomatoes and I am delighted. Gooseberries were very fine and very plentiful this year, so I put up a great many. . . .

I raised a great many flowers and I worked several days in the field. In all I have told about I have had no help but Jerrine. Clyde's mother spends each summer with us, and she helped me with the cooking and the babies. Many of my neighbors did better than I did, although I know many town people would doubt my doing so much, but I did it. I have tried every kind of work this ranch affords, and I can do any of it. Of course I *am* extra strong, but those who try know that strength and knowledge come with doing. I just love to experiment, to work, and to prove out things, so that ranch life and "roughing it" just suit me.

—Elinore Pruitt Stewart

But in the house! I have never anywhere seen such realized possibilities of color! The fine harmonic sense of the woman and artist and poet thrilled through these long chords of color, and filled the room with an atmosphere which made it seem like living in a rainbow. The tops of the low bookcases, that filled all the wall space not opened in windows to the sea, were massed with her beloved flowers. I remember she told me that at four in the morning, when the sea and sky seemed to be spread for her alone, she was always out gathering them. I like to think of her there—the tall, white figure standing under the sky and beside the sea which laps her much-loved Isles of Shoals, among the flowers in the early morning, which, although bare of humanity, she found full to the brim of the beauty which her soul loved.

Later her friends always found her in her room, with books and piano and flowers, making a harmony together which must live in many hearts until Heaven substitutes something as good and without decay. . . .

Everywhere around the room roses were sweeping into depths of roses, and nasturtiums going from palest yellow into winelike claret, and blue of asters into darks of purples, and sweet-peas stood in groups on the tables and by the windows; but my eyes always came back to the soft gradation over the chimney-piece, with the bit of blue sea over the white. Both blue and white were so tender and mixed in quality, and yet so strong in contrast, they might have been born of the bass and treble notes which went floating over them from the great piano.

It was in this room, and enjoying its color as I have enjoyed few things in life, and conscious all the while of its impermanence, conscious that in lastingness of quality it was scarcely more than a dream of color, that I began to think of making a summer dream of it in my garden. It is a summer dream, and yet a reality—not only to me but to other garden lovers; but I still enjoy the remembrance of its source, and shall, perhaps, enjoy it beyond the limits which separate earthly and heavenly gardens.

—CANDACE WHEELER

When our two souls stand up erect and strong,
  Face to face, silent, drawing nigh and nigher,
  Until the lengthening wings break into fire,
  At either curved point,—what bitter wrong
  Can the earth do to us . . .

—ELIZABETH BARRETT BROWNING

Love

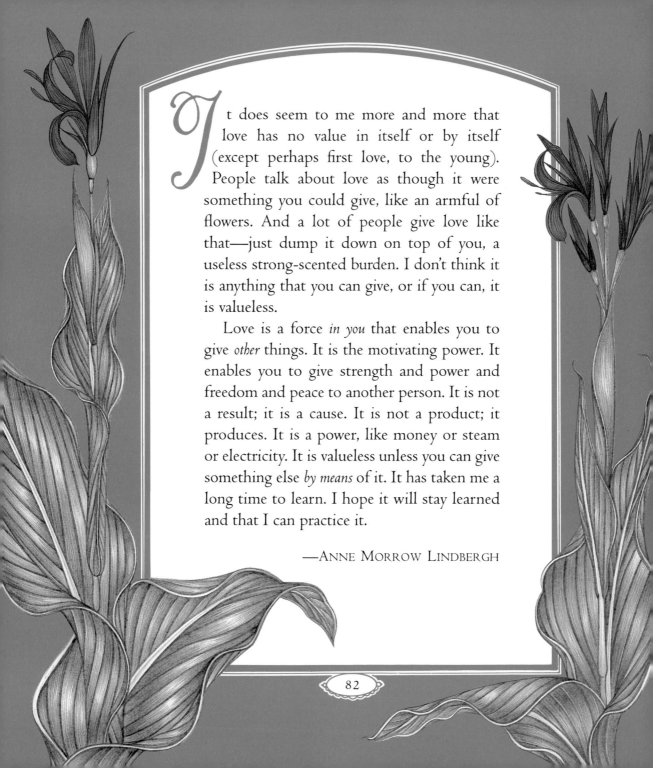

*I*t does seem to me more and more that love has no value in itself or by itself (except perhaps first love, to the young). People talk about love as though it were something you could give, like an armful of flowers. And a lot of people give love like that—just dump it down on top of you, a useless strong-scented burden. I don't think it is anything that you can give, or if you can, it is valueless.

Love is a force *in you* that enables you to give *other* things. It is the motivating power. It enables you to give strength and power and freedom and peace to another person. It is not a result; it is a cause. It is not a product; it produces. It is a power, like money or steam or electricity. It is valueless unless you can give something else *by means* of it. It has taken me a long time to learn. I hope it will stay learned and that I can practice it.

—ANNE MORROW LINDBERGH

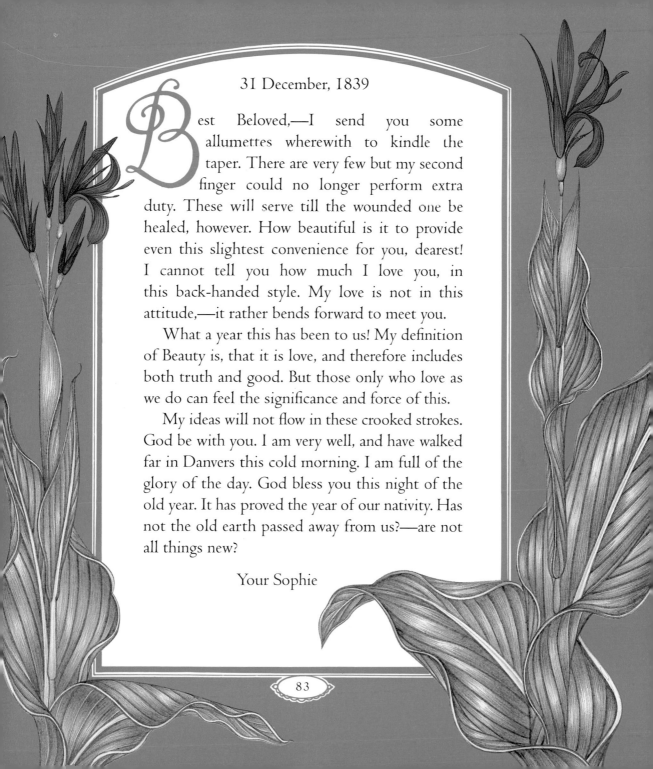

31 December, 1839

Best Beloved,—I send you some allumettes wherewith to kindle the taper. There are very few but my second finger could no longer perform extra duty. These will serve till the wounded one be healed, however. How beautiful is it to provide even this slightest convenience for you, dearest! I cannot tell you how much I love you, in this back-handed style. My love is not in this attitude,—it rather bends forward to meet you.

What a year this has been to us! My definition of Beauty is, that it is love, and therefore includes both truth and good. But those only who love as we do can feel the significance and force of this.

My ideas will not flow in these crooked strokes. God be with you. I am very well, and have walked far in Danvers this cold morning. I am full of the glory of the day. God bless you this night of the old year. It has proved the year of our nativity. Has not the old earth passed away from us?—are not all things new?

Your Sophie

83

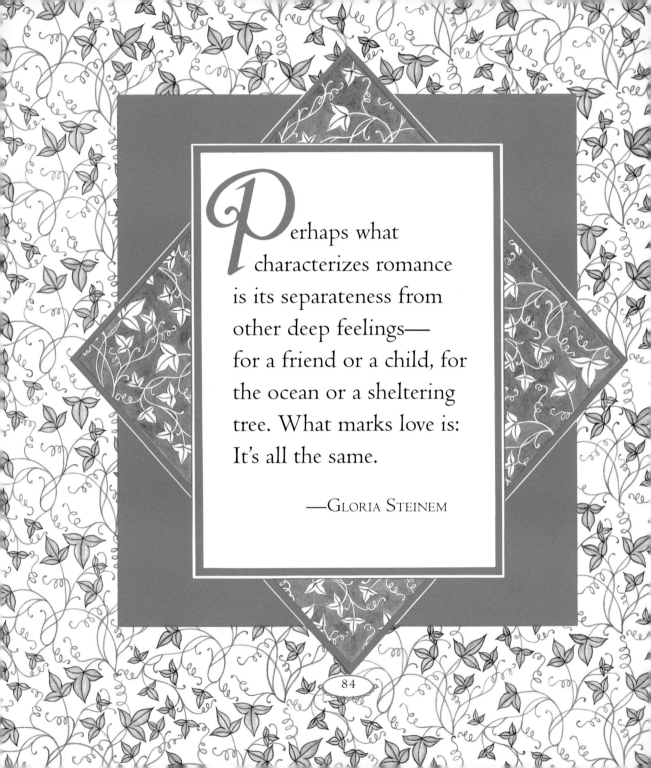

$\mathcal{P}$erhaps what characterizes romance is its separateness from other deep feelings— for a friend or a child, for the ocean or a sheltering tree. What marks love is: It's all the same.

—GLORIA STEINEM

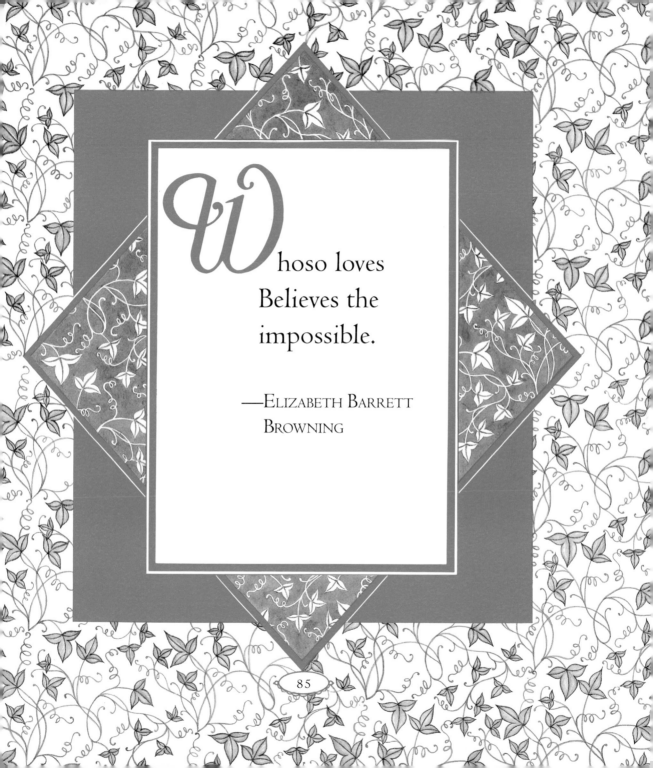

Whoso loves
Believes the
impossible.

—Elizabeth Barrett
Browning

I have learned not to worry about
    love;
but to honor its coming
with all my heart.
To examine the dark mysteries
of the blood
with headless head and
swirl,
to know the rush of feelings
swift and flowing
as water.

The source appears to be
some inexhaustible
spring
within our twin and triple
selves;
the new face I turn up
to you
no one else on earth
has ever
seen.

—ALICE WALKER

I will be the gladdest thing
Under the sun!
I will touch a hundred flowers
And not pick one.

I will look at cliffs and clouds
With quiet eyes,

Watch the wind bow down the grass,
And the grass rise.

And when lights begin to show
Up from the town,
I will mark which must be mine,
And then start down!

—EDNA ST. VINCENT MILLAY

We could never have loved the earth so well if we had had no childhood in it—if it were not the earth where the same flowers come up again every spring that we used to gather with our tiny fingers as we sat lisping to ourselves on the grass—the same hips and haws on the autumn hedgerows—the same red-breasts that we used to call "God's birds," because they did no harm to the precious crops. What novelty is worth that sweet monotony where everything is known, and *loved* because it is known?

The wood I walk in on this mild May day, with the young yellow-brown foliage of the oaks between me and the blue sky, the white star-flowers and the blue-eyed speedwell and the ground ivy at my feet—what grove of tropic palms, what strange ferns or splendid broad-petalled blossoms could ever thrill

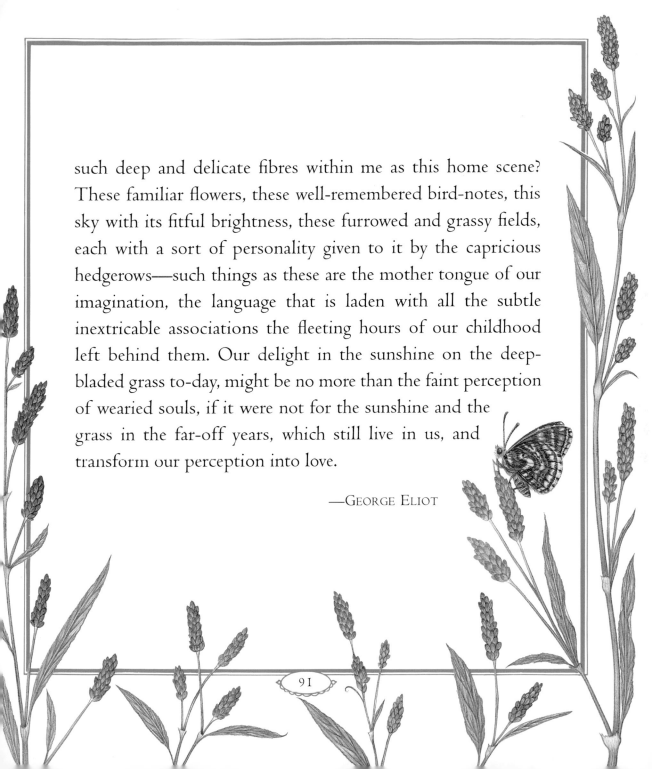

such deep and delicate fibres within me as this home scene? These familiar flowers, these well-remembered bird-notes, this sky with its fitful brightness, these furrowed and grassy fields, each with a sort of personality given to it by the capricious hedgerows—such things as these are the mother tongue of our imagination, the language that is laden with all the subtle inextricable associations the fleeting hours of our childhood left behind them. Our delight in the sunshine on the deep-bladed grass to-day, might be no more than the faint perception of wearied souls, if it were not for the sunshine and the grass in the far-off years, which still live in us, and transform our perception into love.

—GEORGE ELIOT

Of what I have said of her has any meaning
you will believe that her death was the greatest
disaster that could happen; it was as though on
some brilliant day of spring the racing clouds
of a sudden stood still, grew dark, and massed
themselves; the wind flagged, and all creatures on
the earth moaned or wandered seeking aimlessly.
But what figure or variety of figures will do
justice to the shapes which since then she
has taken in countless lives? The dead,
so people say, are forgotten, or they
should rather say, that life has for
the most part little significance to any of us.
But now and again on more occasions than I
can number, in bed at night, or in the street,
or as I come into the room, there she
is; beautiful, emphatic, with her familiar
phrase and her laugh; closer than any of
the living are, lighting our random lives
as with a burning torch, infinitely noble
and delightful to her children.

—VIRGINIA WOOLF

92

*E*ven as we grew up, my mother could not help imposing herself between her children and whatever it was they might take it in mind to reach out for in the world. For she would get it for them, if it was good enough for them—she would have to be very sure—and give it to them, at whatever cost to herself: valiance was in her very fibre. She stood always prepared in herself to challenge the world in our place. She did indeed tend to make the world look dangerous, and so it had been to her. A way had to be found around her love sometimes, without challenging *that*, and at the same time cherishing it in its unassailable strength.

—Eudora Welty

What more shall I say about them? I cannot and need not say much more. In externals, they were two unobtrusive women; a perfectly secluded life gave them retiring manners and habits. In Emily's nature the extremes of vigour and simplicity seemed to meet. Under an unsophisticated culture, inartificial tastes, and an unpretending outside, lay a secret power and fire that might have inflamed the brain and kindled the veins of a hero; but she had no worldly wisdom; her powers were unadapted to the practical business of life; she would fail to defend her most manifest rights, to consult her most legitimate advantage. An interpreter ought always to have stood between her and the world. Her will was not very flexible, and it generally opposed her interest. Her temper was magnanimous, but warm and sudden; her spirit altogether unbending.

Anne's character was milder and more

subdued; she wanted the power, the fire, the originality of her sister, but was well endowed with quiet virtues of her own. Long-suffering, self-denying, reflective, and intelligent, a constitutional reserve and taciturnity placed and kept her in the shade, and covered her mind, and especially her feelings, with a sort of nun-like veil, which was rarely lifted. Neither Emily nor Anne was learned; they had no thought of filling their pitchers at the well-springs of other minds; they always wrote from the impulse of nature, the dictates of intuition, and from such stores of observation as their limited experience had enabled them to amass. I may sum up all by saying, that for strangers they were nothing, for superficial observers less than nothing; but for those who had known them all their lives in the intimacy of close relationship, they were genuinely good and truly great.

—CHARLOTTE BRONTË

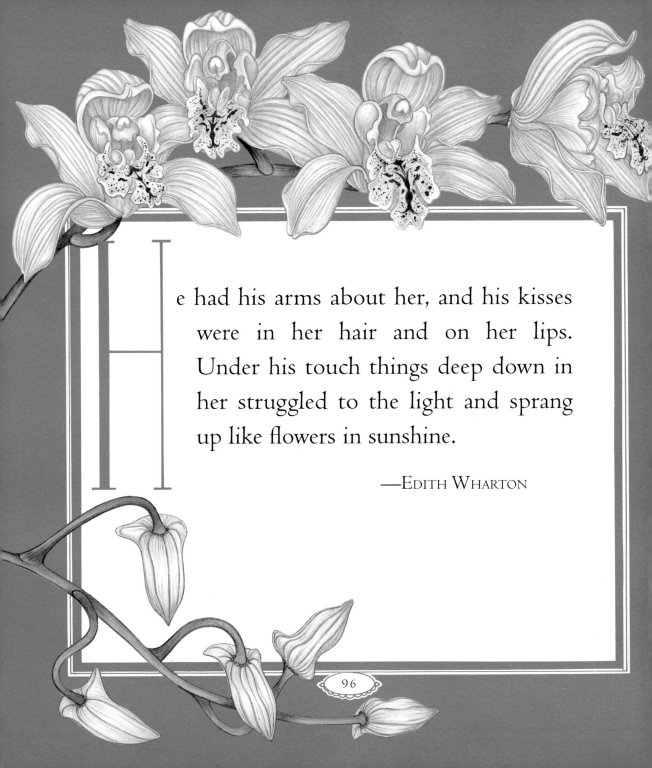

He had his arms about her, and his kisses were in her hair and on her lips. Under his touch things deep down in her struggled to the light and sprang up like flowers in sunshine.

—EDITH WHARTON

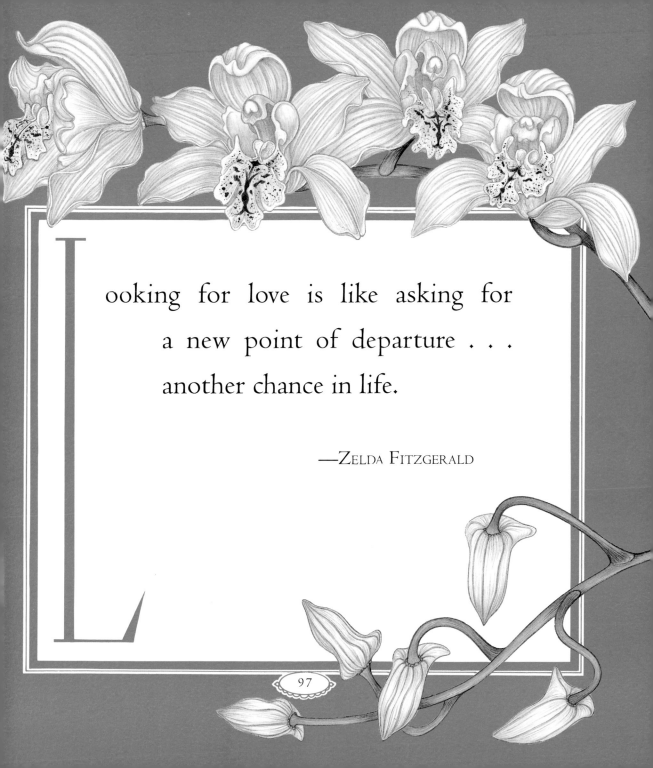

Looking for love is like asking for a new point of departure . . . another chance in life.

—Zelda Fitzgerald

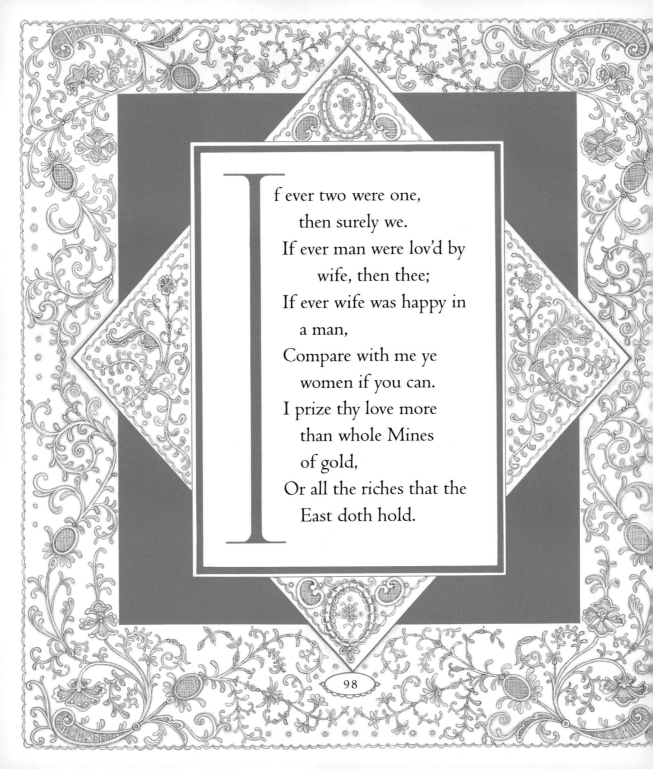

If ever two were one,
then surely we.
If ever man were lov'd by
wife, then thee;
If ever wife was happy in
a man,
Compare with me ye
women if you can.
I prize thy love more
than whole Mines
of gold,
Or all the riches that the
East doth hold.

My love is such that Rivers
    cannot quench,
Nor ought but love from thee,
    give recompence.
Thy love is such I can no
    way repay,
The heavens reward thee
    manifold I pray.
Then while we live, in love
    lets so persever,
That when we live no more,
    we may live ever.

—Anne Bradstreet

99

Each that we lose takes
part of us;
A crescent still abides,
Which like the moon,
some turbid night,
Is summoned by the
tides.

—EMILY DICKINSON

That Love is all there is,
Is all we know of Love;
It is enough, the freight
should be
Proportioned to the
groove.

—EMILY DICKINSON

What greater thing is there for two
human souls than to feel that they
are joined for life—to strengthen
each other in all labour, to rest on
each other in all sorrow, to minister
to each other in all pain . . .

—GEORGE ELIOT

Sleep, darling

> I have a small
> daughter called
> Cleis, who is
>
> like a golden
> flower
>   I wouldn't
> take all Croesus'
> kingdom with love
> thrown in, for her

—Sappho

About the Writers

Annie Dillard (1945–) American writer, author of *Pilgrim at Tinker's Creek* and *An American Childhood.*

Louise Bogan (1897–1970) American poet and essayist, best known for her exquisitely crafted lyrics. A divorcée, she was the mother of a daughter.

Beryl Markham (1902–1986) British aviation pioneer and author of *West With the Night.*

May Sarton (1912–) American poet and novelist, as well as extraordinary diarist, whose published journals about her life deal with questions of identity, pain, and aging, and the nature of creativity.

Sojourner Truth (c. 1797–1883) Former slave and visionary who renamed herself "Sojourner Truth" after mystical voices first spoke to her, and whose religious zeal became inextricably linked to the cause of abolitionism. Encouraged by Elizabeth Cady Stanton, she lectured on behalf of women's suffrage after the Civil War.

Christina Rossetti (1830–1894) English poet who came from a distinguished family of artists: her father was an Italian poet, one brother was an important editor, while the other brother, Dante Gabriel Rossetti, was a Pre-Raphaelite poet and painter. A devout believer in the Anglican Church, she never married the man she loved because he lacked the depth of her faith.

Amy Lowell (1874–1925) American poet who was an innovator in poetic form, as well as an accomplished translator of Japanese and Chinese verse.

Emily Dickinson (1830–1886) American poet who lived a reclusive life and published only seven poems in her lifetime. Her sister discovered more than 1,000 poems after Emily's death, and their posthumous publication assured her position as one of America's greatest poets.

Kate Chopin (1851–1904) American writer, who was happily married to a cotton trader and the mother of six children. Her husband's untimely death when she was thirty-two devastated her, but also propelled her into writing. *The Awakening,* published in 1899, is an extraordinary novel of independence, way ahead of its time.

George Eliot (pseudonym of Mary Anne Evans) (1819–1880) English novelist who defied convention by living with George Henry Lewes, a married man who could not obtain a divorce. She wrote under a man's name to distinguish her work from the popular romances written by women; her first book, *Adam Bede,* established her reputation. After Lewes's death, she married a man twenty years younger than she.

Muriel Rukeyser (1913–1980) American poet and activist whose published works included prose and children's books.

Maya Angelou (1928–   ) African-American writer whose autobiographical works, including *I Know Why the Caged Bird Sings,* have moved and instructed untold thousands of women.

Karen Horney (1885–1952) German-born American psychotherapist who founded the American Institute of Psychoanalysis.

H. D. (Hilda Doolittle) (1886–1961) American poet who emigrated to England, where she wrote and lived out her life. Broadly influenced and inspired by the Greek poet Sappho, she translated Greek plays and wrote prose as well as verse.

Anne Frank (1929–1945) German-born Jewish diarist whose diary, written in Dutch, recounting the two years spent in hiding from the Gestapo during the German occupation of the Netherlands, is not only a moving portrait of a young girl's entry into womanhood but a testament to the human spirit. She died of typhus in Bergen-Belsen. Her father found the diary amid the papers in the annex where they lived, and had it published.

Margaret Fuller (1810–1850) American journalist and early feminist. Upon her untimely death, Elizabeth Barrett Browning called her the epitome of truth and courage.

Emily Brontë (1818–1848) English novelist and poet who wrote the classic *Wuthering Heights,* first published (as was the work of her sisters, Anne and Charlotte) under a male pseudonym.

Kim Chernin (1940–   ) American writer of nonfiction whose works include *The Hungry Self, In My Mother's House,* and *Reinventing Eve.*

Madeleine L'Engle (1918–   ) American author of children's books (among them the classic *A Wrinkle in Time,* winner of the Newbery Medal) as well as adult nonfiction. She is the mother of three children.

Elizabeth Bishop (1911–1979) American poet, winner of the Pulitzer Prize for poetry in 1955, whose mentor and friend was another poet, Marianne Moore.

Charlotte Mew (1869–1928) English writer of poems and short stories whose work was admired by male contemporaries, among them Thomas Hardy and Walter de la Mare, but who died in obscurity. Raised in a Victorian household, she nonetheless lived an unconventional life.

Chao Li-hua (?–?) A poet of the Chinese Ming dynasty (1368–1644) about whom nothing, save her work, is known.

Anne Morrow Lindbergh (1906–   ) American writer whose diaries and letters *(Bring Me a Unicorn, Hour of Gold, Hour of Lead, Locked Rooms and Open Doors)* and her classic *Gift from the Sea* have captivated readers for nearly four decades. The daughter of an ambassador, she married an American hero, Charles Lindbergh. After the tragic kidnapping and murder of her first child, she went on to bear and raise five children.

Amelia Earhart (1897–1937) American aviator, the first woman to cross the Atlantic by plane in 1928 and, in 1932, the first to cross it alone. She was lost at sea while attempting an around-the-world flight. Married to publisher G. P. Putnam, she had no children.

Takashina Kishi (?–996) Japanese poet who was the wife of a powerful politician and the mother of three, one of whom became deputy minister. Indeed, she is commonly known as *Gidosanshi no ha ha* ("mother of the deputy minister").

Harriet Tubman (c. 1820–1913) American abolitionist who, as a slave, escaped in 1849 and then worked on the Underground Railroad, bringing more than 300 slaves to their freedom.

Marge Piercy (1936–   ) American writer and poet, and activist in the feminist movement.

Adrienne Rich (1929–   ) American poet and activist whose prose work *Of Woman Born* is a classic in the field of women's writing about women.

Hanna Rion (1875–?) American garden writer who wrote at the beginning of this century.

Anna Akhmatova (pseudonym of Anna Gorenko) (1889–1966) Russian poet who wrote on both personal themes as well as political ones, among them poems commemorating Joseph Stalin's victims. Married to and later divorced from a poet who was executed for his political views, she was unable to publish her works for eighteen years, and worked as a translator.

Elinore Pruitt Stewart (1878–1933) American homesteader who, alone with her daughter (she was widowed), set out for Wyoming in 1909. *Letters of a Woman Homesteader* is the chronicle of her experience and triumph in the American wilderness.

Candace Wheeler (1827–1923) American designer of fabrics and tapestries who was also known for her salon for contemporary painters at her beautiful home. Among her books are *Principles of Home Design* and *Yesterdays in a Busy Life*, an autobiography.

Sophia Peabody Hawthorne (1809–1871) American, best known as the wife of Nathaniel Hawthorne, author of *The Scarlet Letter*. Their marriage was a marriage of true minds; of her, he wrote, "My wife is, in the strictest sense, my sole companion, and I need no other. There is no vacancy in my mind any more than in my heart."

Gloria Steinem (1934–   ) American feminist, publisher, and writer; author of, among other works, *Revolution from Within.*

Elizabeth Barrett Browning (1806–1861) English poet who lived much of her early life as a semi-invalid. Her volume of poetry was a favorite of the poet Robert Browning, with whom she first corresponded, then met and fell in love with. Their courtship was kept a secret from her tyrannical father, but they eloped and went to live in Italy, where, supported by her happy marriage, she regained her health and bore a son.

Alice Walker (1944–   ) African-American writer, poet, and novelist whose works include *The Color Purple* and *In Search of Our Mother's Gardens.*

Edna St. Vincent Millay (1892–1950) American lyric poet who achieved renown at a young age for both her writing and her bohemian life.

Virginia Woolf (1882–1941) English novelist and essayist and cofounder, with her husband, Leonard Woolf, of the Hogarth Press. Subject to breakdowns after her mother's death when she was a girl (and probably after sexual abuse by a relative), she endured periodic mental illness throughout her life. She committed suicide before the onset of what she feared would be a new attack.

Eudora Welty (1909–   ) American writer of short stories and nonfiction who, apart from her years at college, has lived all her life in Jackson, Mississippi. She won the Pulitzer Prize in 1972.

Charlotte Brontë (1816–1855) English author of *Jane Eyre*, among other titles, and one of three gifted sisters who were originally published under male pseudonyms. Her sister Emily wrote *Wuthering Heights.*

Edith Wharton (1862–1937) American writer, author of poetry, short stories, essays, and novels. Born into wealth, she was educated abroad, made her debut "into society," and, at twenty-three, married. The marriage was childless and unhappy, and eventually ended in divorce. In her later, intensely productive years, she lived in Europe.

Zelda Fitzgerald (1900–1948) American author of *Save Me the Waltz*, best known as the wife of writer F. Scott Fitzgerald, to whose work her own writings and diaries contributed significantly.

Anne Bradstreet (1612–1672) The first great American poet (as well as the first American woman poet). Happily married and the mother of eight children, she wrote most movingly on domestic themes.

Sappho (c. 610–c. 580 B.C.) One of the great lyric poets of Western antiquity, who often wrote on love, Sappho was married and the mother of a daughter, Cleis.